Dragons! The Musical

Words by Nick Toczek
Music by Malcolm Singer
Edited by Christopher Hussey & Ann Farmer

A dramatic and comical new musical for Key Stages 2 and 3, offering scope to include younger children and adults. **Dragons!** contains nine original, varied and challenging songs, with optional solos and instrumentals. It comes with a rhyming play, also suitable for Key Stages 2 and 3, or the songs can simply be sung as a song cycle for choirs.

Duration: approximately 45 minutes
TEACHER'S BOOK with CD

No musical expertise is required as the CD contains demonstration and backing tracks – all the music you will need to rehearse and perform the songs.

TEACHER'S BOOK complete with CD, production notes and music
The script and song lyrics are in the separate Pupil's Book GA11638

A licence should be obtained from the publishers for performances of this work.

SONGS
The Dragon's Curse 4
Being A Dragon (including Musical Interlude I) 7
The Child Who Pretended To Be A Dragon 13
The Dragon Who Ate Our School 17
Finding A Dragon's Lair 25
Speaking Dragonese 30
The Strength Of Dragons 37
Dragons Everywhere 43
Musical Interlude II 51
The Dragon's Curse Reprise 54

Anyone considering mounting a full-scale production of this musical might like to know that (a) Malcolm Singer and Nick Toczek have several more dragon songs available for inclusion, and (b) Nick Toczek would be willing to add new scenes and/or lengthen existing scenes to incorporate these additional songs. To contact Nick Toczek, email him at slaphead@1000rpm.freeserve.co.uk, and Malcolm Singer can be contacted via the 'Feedback' link on his website www.malcolmsinger.co.uk.

Golden Apple Productions
part of The Music Sales Group
London / New York / Paris / Sydney / Copenhagen / Berlin / Madrid / Tokyo

MALCOLM SINGER is a composer and conductor, director of music at the Yehudi Menuhin School, and a professor of composition at the Guildhall School of Music and Drama in London. He read music at Magdalene College, Cambridge before studying in Europe with both Nadia Boulanger and Gyorgy Ligeti. He was later awarded a Harkness Fellowship, spending two years at Stanford University, California, and was director of music of London's Zemel Choir for ten years.

In 1995, a 'portrait' concert of his music was given in Cologne, and in 2003 there was a 50th birthday concert of his music given in St John's, Smith Square, London.

Malcolm has worked with young musicians throughout his professional life, and has composed much music for young performers, as well as for both amateur and professional musicians.

NICK TOCZEK is a best-selling writer and performer who lives in Bradford, where he was born in 1950. As a poet, storyteller, professional magician, stand-up comic, puppeteer, public speaker and vocalist with bands, he has given more than 40,000 public performances.

As an author, he has published over two dozen books since 1972. His poetry books alone have sold well over 300,000 copies. For children, he has published numerous poetry collections, a musical and a pantomime. For adults, he has published poetry and short story collections, novels and CDs. His poems have been used in television and radio ads, on CBBC and in catatas.

He presents his own weekly local radio show, has worked as a visiting writer in more than 4,000 schools, and regularly appears on radio and television. His work also features in the new BBC Digital Curriculum for primary schools.

Published by
Golden Apple Productions
8/9 Frith Street, London W1D 3JB, England.

Exclusive Distributors:
Music Sales Limited
Distribution Centre, Newmarket Road, Bury St Edmunds, Suffolk IP33 3YB, England.
Music Sales Corporation
257 Park Avenue South, New York, NY10010, United States of America.
Music Sales Pty Limited
120 Rothschild Avenue, Rosebery, NSW 2018, Australia.

Order No. GA11627
ISBN 1-84449-480-2
This book © Copyright 2005 by Golden Apple Productions.

Unauthorised reproduction of any part of this publication by any means including photocopying is an infringement of copyright.

A licence should be obtained from the publishers for performances of this work.

Cover design by Butterworth Design
Music & text processed by Camden Music
Printed in Great Britain

Your Guarantee of Quality
As publishers, we strive to produce every book to the highest commercial standards.
The music has been freshly engraved and the book has been carefully designed to minimise awkward page turns and to make playing from it a real pleasure. Particular care has been given to specifying acid-free, neutral-sized paper made from pulps which have not been elemental chlorine bleached. This pulp is from farmed sustainable forests and was produced with special regard for the environment. Throughout, the printing and binding have been planned to ensure a sturdy, attractive publication which should give years of enjoyment.
If your copy fails to meet our high standards, please inform us and we will gladly replace it.

www.musicsales.com

DRAGONS!

Cast:

Fergus: a boy who's convinced he's turning into a dragon.

His family:
Mum: Fergus's couch-potato mother
Dad: Fergus's couch-potato dad

His six imaginary mates:
Kid A: scared
Kid B: copycat
Kid C: bully
Kid D: rude
Kid E: bigheaded
Kid F: badly-done-by

In his school:
First Voice: Fergus's phantom headteacher (who's heard but never seen)
Extra Class Mates: enough other dragon kids to make up a full class
Second Voice: Fergus's phantom language teacher (also heard but not seen)

Characters from his early childhood:
Mrs Meacher: gym teacher
Gordon: traffic warden
Mrs Ritter: babysitter
Mervyn: mouse-catcher
Miss McPeake: shop-keeper
The neighbours: as few or as many as you like

Author's suggestions

1. First Voice & Second Voice. I suggest an off-stage microphone for these two, ideally with slight echo (which can be achieved by simply having them speak into a metal dustbin or rubbish bin!). N.B. Because neither of these actually appear onstage, they don't have to learn their words, they can just read them from the script.

2. Fergus + Kids A–F. If more parts are wanted and/or less demanding parts for the key players, these characters could be played by different (older/larger) actors once they become dragons. Thus scenes 1,2 & 7 would go to one set of players, and scenes 3–6 to a second set of actors. If all simply wore a t-shirt with their names on, this would avoid confusing the audience.

3. Fergus. For scene 3, he doesn't need to learn his lines, he can simply read them from the 'menu'. And in scene 5 he (and the kids) can do the same, with scripts in their schoolbooks.

4. Fergus. In scene 2, his wings are rudimentary, only noticeable when he turns round. All it needs is wing-shaped card with feathers glued on one side, a coat-hanger or hook taped onto the other side so it can be hooked into his collar.

THE DRAGON'S CURSE

BEING A DRAGON / MUSICAL INTERLUDE I

Musical Interlude I

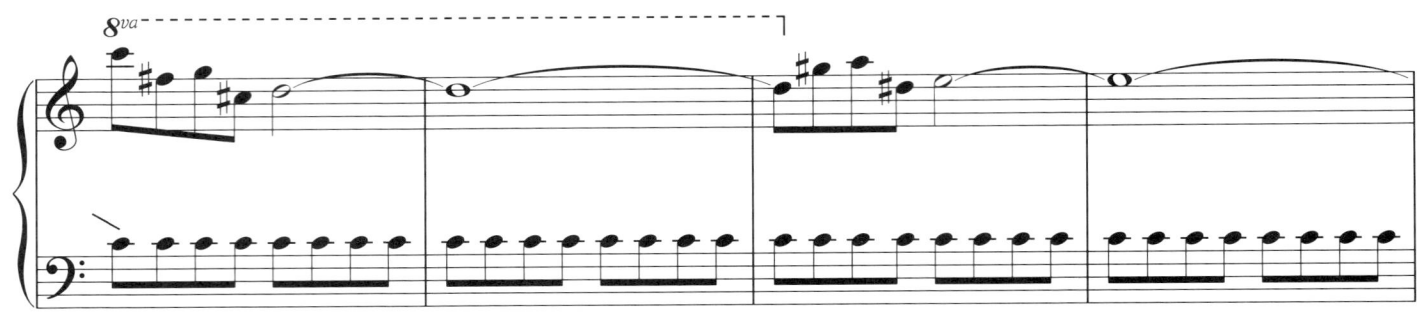

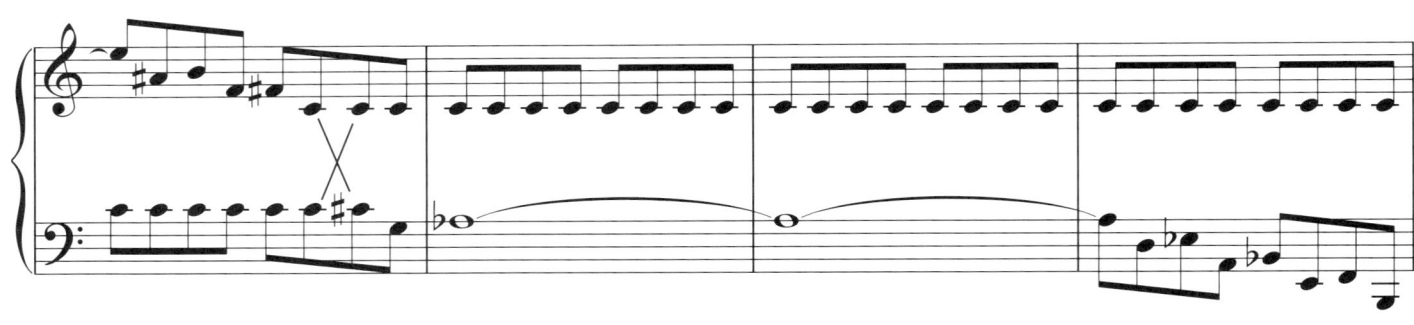

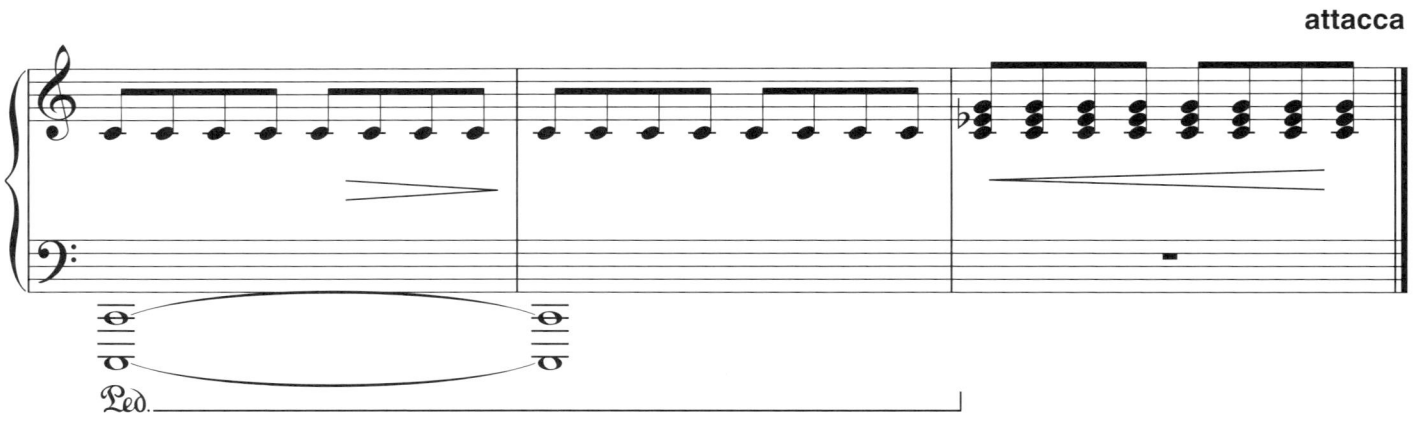

THE CHILD WHO PRETENDED TO BE A DRAGON

THE DRAGON WHO ATE OUR SCHOOL

FINDING A DRAGON'S LAIR

SPEAKING DRAGONESE

THE STRENGTH OF DRAGONS

Very aggressively and always loud!

♩ = c.132

All them drag-ons, 'ard as nails,

bend steel gir-ders wi' their tails.

Green in Eng-land, red in Wales,

'omes in caves and dun-geon jails reek of smoke and old ent-rails,

'oard-ing gold and guard-ing grails, wing-span wide as gal-leon sails.

All them drag-ons, tough as bricks,

'atched from eggs, like nest-ling chicks, eyes as cold as old oil-slicks. Van-dal-is-ing lun-at-ics, they knock whole vil-lag-es for six, 'ead-butt cas-tle walls for kicks and smash 'em up like match-sticks.

All them drag-ons, built like boots, bul-let-proof in scal-y suits, are cruel and cal-cul-at-ing brutes. Night-time flights down sec-ret routes to meet up cos they're in ca-hoots.

Vile and vic-ious in dis-putes, they share nef-ar-i-ous pur-suits.

All them drag-ons, rough as rocks, an-arch-ic and un-orth-od-ox, 'ave bod-y parts like con-crete blocks. Each 'as a gob-o'-teeth that locks like

thief-proof vault or strong-box. These beasts gang up in flam-ing flocks and

ar-moured knights are laugh-ing stocks.

All them drag-ons, 'ard as nails.

DRAGONS EVERYWHERE

♩ = c.125

Miss-us Meach-er, our gym teach-er, looks at you like she might eat-cha.
Miss-us Rit-ter, ba-by-sit-ter, T. V. watch-er, sil-ent knit-ter.

An-ger al-ters ev-'ry feat-ure. She be-comes an-oth-er creat-ure,
I know why her clothes don't fit her. She's an-oth-er fi-re spit-ter,

cresc.

winged av - en - ger, scream - er, screech - er. Her
beast - ly bat - tle - scarred and bit - ter.

f

Burn - ing breath, much more than warm; she blis - ters pup - ils in her form. If
bat - like wings have both been shorn, but I know that she's drag - on's spawn. If

she's a hum - an, I'm a un - i - corn.
she's a hum - an, I'm a un - i - corn.

mf

Then there's Gord - on,
Mouse - man Mer - vyn,

mp

traf - fic ward - en.___ Ord - in - ar - y, dull with bore - dom,
dressed in rat - skin,___ brings his traps in, catch - es ver - min,

'til he roared 'n' ripped 'n' clawed 'n' ran a - mok, all light - ning jawed 'n'
scratch - es his rep - til - i - an chin, his fin - ger nails are long and thin, his

cresc.

flam - ing tongued 'n' toothed and clawed 'n' Fright - en - ing as a thun - der - storm.___
blood - shot eyes, his ev - il grin; a twist - ed fig - ure, worn and torn,___

f

Un - der - neath his u - ni - form if
who can't re - call where he was born, if

f

45

there's a hum-an, I'm a u-ni-corn.
he's a hum-an, I'm a u-ni-corn.

Miss Mc-Peake, our glum shop-keep-er, av-ar-i-cious treas-ure-heap-er, piles 'em high and sells 'em cheap-er. Peo-ple serv-er and floor-sweep-er, deep down, though, she'd be Grim Reap-er.

Cus-tom-ers all sense her scorn. One day they'll meet her with claws drawn. If she's a hum-an, I'm a u-ni-corn.

The fam-il-y that live next-door

seem quite al-right, but night-ly roar

and smoke-stains ru-in their dec-or, and

each of them's a car-niv-ore, I've seen them eat-ing meat that's raw.

cresc.

A moun-tain cave on the Mat-ter-horn

where each first saw the light of dawn. If they are hum-an, I'm a u-ni-corn.

molto rall. **Slow**

And as for me, I'm feel-ing strange, all aches and pains and bad mig-ranes. Soon parts of me -'ll start to change, my limbs and bod-y re-ar-range, and I'll be-come quite dang-er-ous, grow rows of teeth like rose-bush thorns and skin as tough as rhi-no horn, and

Slower still   **Tempo 1**

be a drag-on, not a u-ni-corn.

MUSICAL INTERLUDE II

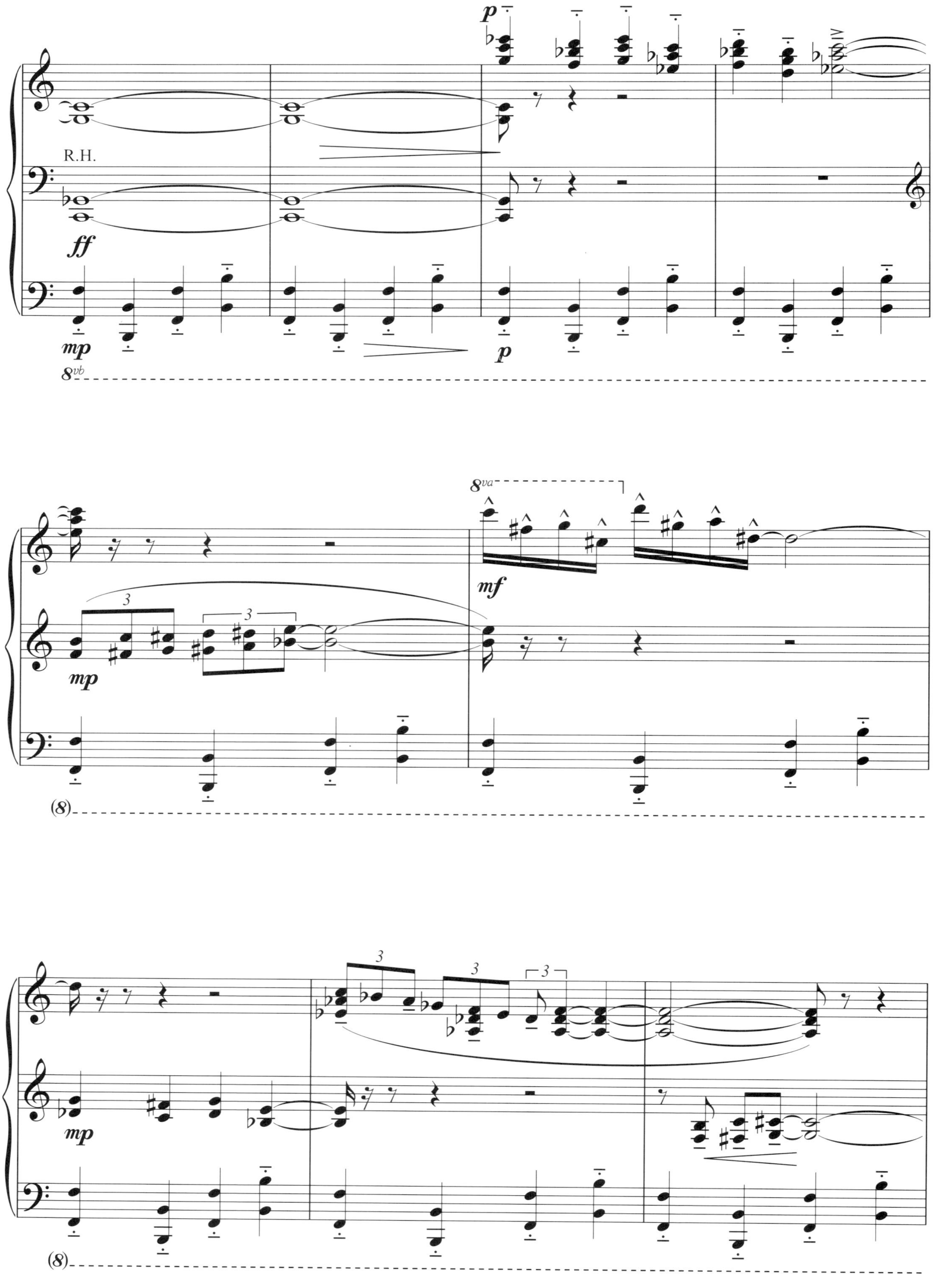
p
R.H.
ff
mp
p
8vb
8va
mf
mp
(8)
mp
(8)

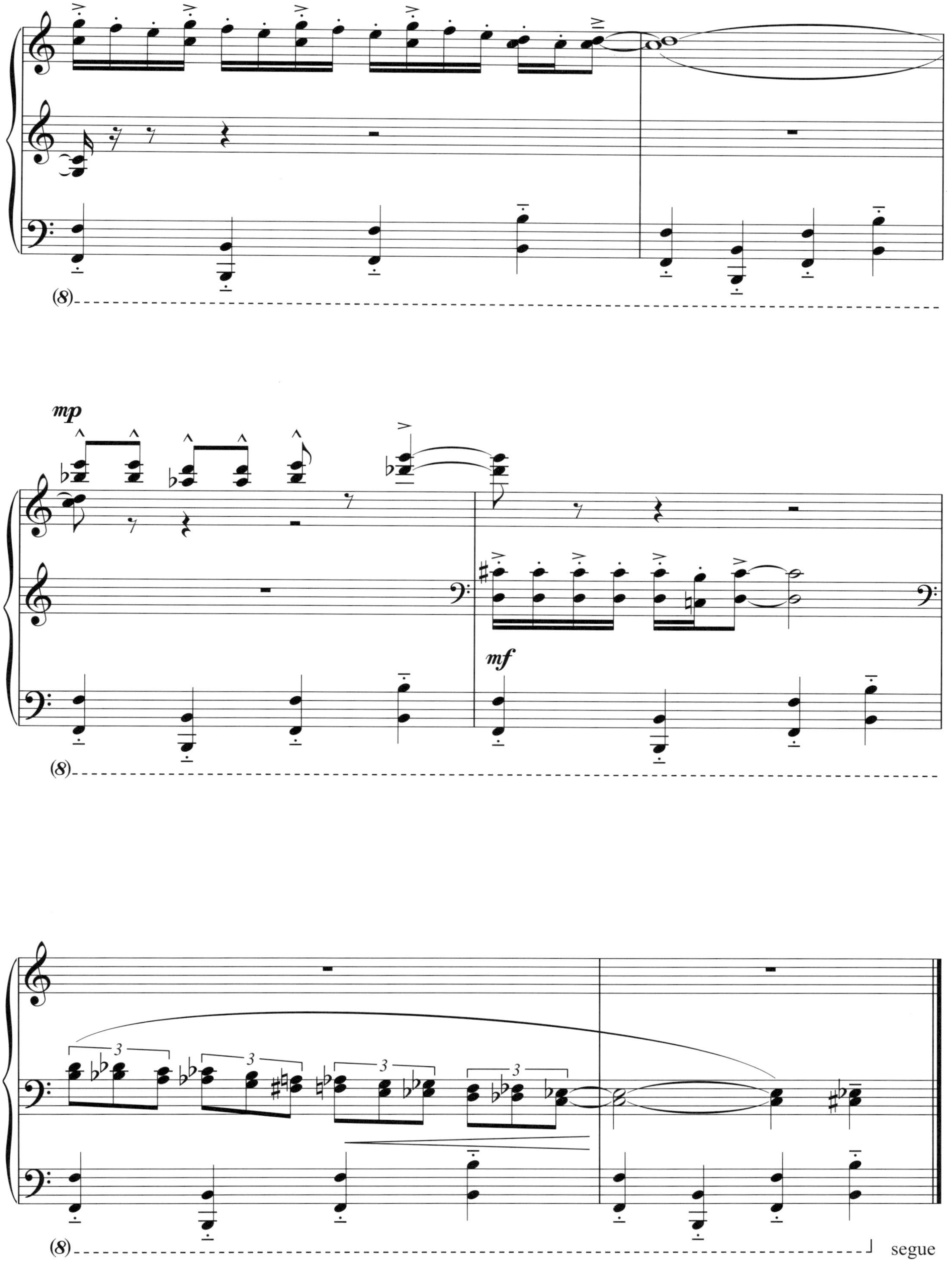
(8)
mp
(8)
mf
(8)
segue

THE DRAGON'S CURSE (REPRISE)

Slow, solemn and portentous (with an ominous air!)

♩ = 60

Ent - er dark - ness. Leave the light.

Here be night - mare. Here be fright. Here be drag - on, flame and flight.

Ent - er dark - ness. Leave the light

p
Earth and wat - er, fire and air. Pre - pare to meet a
pp
Ped.
creat - ure rare. Ent - er, now, if you dare. Ent - er, now, the
dim.
mf
drag - on's lair! The
dim. poco a poco
3

drag - - - on's

lair!